AF438920

How Did You Meet?

I Talk You Talk Press

Copyright © 2021 I Talk You Talk Press

ISBN: 978-4-909733-83-2

www.italkyoutalk.com

info@italkyoutalk.com

All rights reserved. No part of this publication may be resold, reproduced, stored in retrieval system, copied in any form or by any means, electronic, mechanical, photocopying, recording or otherwise transmitted without the prior written permission from the publisher. You must not circulate this publication in any format, online or otherwise.

This is a work of fiction. Names, characters, businesses, organizations, products, places, events and incidents are either the products of the author's imagination or are used in a fictitious manner. We have no affiliation with any existing companies mentioned in this story. Any resemblance to actual persons, living or dead, existing stories or actual events is purely coincidental.

Although the author and publisher have made every effort to ensure that the contents of this book were correct at press time, the author and publisher do not assume and hereby disclaim any liability to any party for any loss, damage, or disruption caused by errors or omissions, whether such errors or omissions result from negligence, accident, or any other cause.

For more information, see the Copyright Notice on our website.

The cover illustration contains images from Adobe for which we have purchased the appropriate license.
Image copyright: © Drobot Dean #276364764 Adobe Stock Standard License

CONTENTS

I Talk You Talk Press

1. JUNE AND WINSTON

June is a university student, but one year, she could not go to classes. June's city had tough rules for Covid19.

Her teachers emailed work for her to do at home. Sometimes her teachers taught online classes. June studied hard, but it was quiet in her small apartment. She missed her friends.

June talked to her mother on Zoom every week. Her mother worried about June.

She is alone in her apartment all day. She must be lonely. It is not good for a young person to be alone. But I can't go to visit her, and she can't come home.

One Friday, June got up late.

Another boring day, she thought. *What can I eat today?* She looked in the refrigerator. *No food!* She looked in the cupboard. *I have rice and noodles, but I have no other food. I have to go to the supermarket.*

It was OK to go to the supermarket to buy food, but she had to wear a mask. Only 20 shoppers were allowed inside the supermarket. Julie had to stand in a line and wait. Every time one shopper came out, another shopper could go in.

Winston makes computer games. He works on his computer every day. It is easy for him to work from home. When the city made tough rules for Covid19, Winston was not worried. *This is easy,* he thought. *My life will not change.*

One Friday, Winston got out of bed. *I have a lot to buy today,* he thought. *I need coffee. I need peanut butter. I want doughnuts.*

He took his backpack and helmet. He left his apartment and ran down the stairs to the bike shed. He unlocked his bike and rode towards the supermarket. Suddenly he thought, *My mask! I don't have my mask!*

He rode back to his apartment and found his mask next to his computer. It was 10:30am when he got to the supermarket and joined the line of people waiting to go in. The line was long, but Winston didn't mind. There was a young woman standing in front of him. She was wearing jeans, boots and a pink jacket. She had long blonde hair. He could not see her face, but Winston thought she looked cute.

I haven't had a girlfriend in a long time. What is her name? Does she have a boyfriend?

A shopper came out of the supermarket. The first person in the line went in, and everyone moved one space closer to the door.

I want to talk to her, thought Winston.

"Hi," he said loudly. "We are waiting a long time today."

June turned around. "Hi," she said. "Yes, we are waiting a long time, but I have to buy some food. And it is quiet in my apartment. It is good to be outside."

"I often work from home. Covid life is not so strange for me." said Winston. "And sometimes I ride my bike in the park. But today I have to buy coffee, peanut butter and doughnuts. What is your job?"

"I am a student, but I can't go to my university. I study at home. What is your job?"

"I make computer games," said Winston.

"Wow!" June was interested. "I love computer games. When I don't want to study anymore, I play computer games. What games do you make?"

"I made a game called Milky Wars. But maybe you don't know it."

"I know Milky Wars! I love it!"

Winston was very happy. "I am pleased you like it. Now I am making a new game. It is called Under Over Rover."

"When can I download it?" asked June.

"It will be a long time. When I finish making it, it will be tested many times. Maybe you can download it next year."

"I will wait, and I will look for Under Over Rover on the Internet. But I hope I can go to classes next year," said June.

While June and Winston were talking, the line was moving closer to the door of the supermarket.

"I can send you a message when my new game is finished," said

Winston.

"OK. Thank you," said June. "I will give you my phone number." She took her smartphone out of her pocket. Winston held his phone up, but they could not exchange numbers. Two metres was too far for the message to travel.

Winston had an idea. He found a piece of paper in his pocket. He had a pen too. He wrote his phone number on the paper in big letters. Then he wrote, 'Please call me'. He held the paper up.

June took a photograph of the paper. "Yes," she said. "I will call you."

A week later, June talked to her mother on Zoom. June's mother was very surprised. June was smiling. She was very happy.

"I have a new boyfriend!" she said. "His name is Winston. He makes computer games. I think he is very famous. He likes bike riding. He is very nice. I see him every day."

June's mother was very angry. "June!" she said. "You can't go out with people. How did you meet him? It is not safe! You can't have a boyfriend. Are you crazy?"

June laughed. "I met him in a line at the supermarket. We were two metres apart. I was wearing a mask. He was wearing a mask. I didn't see his face until we talked on Zoom. We are two metre lovers. But one day we will go on a date."

2. LYDIA AND IVAN

It was Friday evening, and Lydia and her friend Bronwen were leaving work. They worked in the office of a big insurance company.

"Do you have any plans for this weekend?" Bronwen asked Lydia.

"Nothing special. I will clean my apartment, wash my clothes and go to the gym. Do you have any plans?"

Bronwen said, "Oh yes! I have big plans for Saturday night. I am meeting a new guy. He is taking me to eat at that new restaurant, Mickie's. They have a band and dancing on Saturday nights." Lydia was not surprised. She was quiet and shy, but Bronwen was very friendly, and she was not shy. She was always meeting new people.

"How did you meet him?" she asked.

Bronwen laughed. "I have never met him. He is a friend of my brother, Ned. They worked together in Scotland. His name is Ivan and he has come to London for a new job. He doesn't know anyone here, so Ned gave him my phone number and told him to call me. He has a nice voice on the phone, but I guess it's a blind date."

By 6:30pm on Saturday, Lydia was tired. Her apartment was very clean and all her clothes were washed and ironed. She had been to the gym.

I'll order a pizza and watch TV tonight, she thought. *I need a nice quiet evening.*

Then her phone rang. She looked at the screen. It was Bronwen.

"Hi, Bronwen," she said.

"Hi! Get dressed. You're going out tonight!" Bronwen was excited.

"What? I'm tired and you have a date."

"No! We have a date! Ivan called me. He wants to bring a friend. His friend's name is Caleb. It will be a double blind date! You have to come. It will be fun. We'll meet them at the entrance to Mickie's at seven thirty. Don't be late!"

Bronwen hung up.

Lydia looked at her phone and sighed. *I don't want to go out. I don't want to meet a strange man. But I can never say 'no' to Bronwen.*

She did her hair and makeup and put on her favourite dress. It was pale blue with a big skirt. *I am shy, but I love to dance, so maybe tonight won't be so bad. Bronwen talks a lot so maybe I won't have to talk with a strange man.*

Lydia took a taxi to Mickie's. Bronwen was waiting at the door with two men. She was wearing a very short red dress with straps.

"Lydia. This is Ned's friend. His name is Ivan. And this is Caleb," she said.

"Hi," said Lydia. Ivan was very tall. He had big brown eyes and untidy brown hair. *He looks kind,* thought Lydia. Caleb was much shorter. He had black hair and bright green eyes. He looked very cheerful.

"Hi, Lydia," he said. "Thank you for being my date tonight. Bronwen says they have a band, and we can dance. I hope you like dancing."

The restaurant was very crowded and noisy. The food was good. Lydia was pleased because Caleb and Bronwen talked all the time, so she didn't have to think of things to say.

After dinner they danced. Caleb was a very good dancer. *He's a nice friendly man,* thought Lydia. *He is good fun, but I wouldn't like to be his girlfriend. It doesn't matter. This is just a blind date.*

After a while, the band had a rest. They went back to their table to have a drink.

"I need to go to the Ladies' Room," said Bronwen. "Please come with me, Lydia. I want you to help me fix my hair."

In the Ladies' Room, Lydia said, "What's wrong with your hair? It looks OK."

"It is OK," laughed Bronwen. "I wanted to talk to you. Ivan is a very nice man. I like him, but he is a terrible dancer. I saw you and Caleb dancing. He dances very well. Will you dance with Ivan for a while?"

"OK," said Lydia. "I guess that's OK."

When the band started playing again, Bronwen jumped up. "Let's change partners," she said. "Dance with me, Caleb!"

Lydia and Ivan were sitting at the table. Lydia was looking at the tablecloth. She felt very shy.

"Er, I am not a very good dancer, but will you dance with me?"

Lydia looked up. Ivan was smiling at her. *He is so nice and so handsome,* she thought.

She didn't know what to say so she stood up. Ivan took her hand and they walked onto the dance floor. Bronwen was right. Ivan was not a good dancer, and he didn't talk, but he put his arms around Lydia and she put her head on his shoulder. *This is dreamy,* she thought. *But Ivan is Bronwen's date!*

They changed partners again when the band had a rest. Then it was midnight and time to go home. They took a taxi. The first stop was Lydia's apartment building.

Caleb didn't ask for Lydia's phone number. She wasn't unhappy. *He is a nice guy. He is fun. I think he would be a good friend, but not a boyfriend.*

It was early on Sunday morning when Lydia's phone woke her up.

She looked at the screen. She didn't know the number. *Who is this? Should I answer it? Is it safe?*

She was too tired to think. So she pushed the green button.

"Yes?" she said sleepily.

"Uh, hello. This is Ivan."

"What? Why are you calling me?"

"I thought maybe we could meet for coffee today," said Ivan.

"But Ivan! We can't! Bronwen is my friend. You were her date last night!"

"I think we can," said Ivan. "After the taxi went to your apartment, it went to my apartment. Then Caleb and Bronwen were alone in the taxi. They decided they liked each other very much. Caleb called me this morning and asked me if it was OK. Of course I said 'yes'. Bronwen is a great person, but I like you much more. So I called Bronwen to get your phone number."

"Oh! OK. I would love to meet you for coffee."

Lydia got out of bed. She went to the kitchen to make coffee. *Ivan is wonderful. He is not perfect. No one is perfect. I wonder if I can teach him to dance?*

3. GISELLE AND KEITH

Giselle loves fashion. Every day before she goes to work, she chooses an outfit. She plans the clothes, shoes, accessories and makeup. Giselle works in a school office. The teachers don't like Giselle's style. They think it is strange. But Giselle is a very good worker, so they don't say anything.

One day, Giselle leaves the school office to go to the post office. She wants to send some letters. Today her hair is pink. She is wearing red boots and a silver skirt.

A man stops her in the street. "Excuse me," he says. "I work for the newspaper. The newspaper has a section called 'Street Fashion'. I like your style. Can I take a picture to put in the newspaper?"

Giselle is very happy. "Yes! You can take a picture of me."

The young man takes a photograph. "I am sure your picture will be in the newspaper tomorrow. Please look."

The next day, Giselle buys a newspaper. She looks for the section called 'Street Fashion'. Her picture is there! She is very excited. Under her picture it says, ---*'Photograph taken by Milt Pearce'*---.

Giselle calls the newspaper office. She asks to speak to Milt Pearce. "I want a digital copy of my photograph," she says. "Can you email a copy to my computer?"

"No, I can't do that," says Milt. "Maybe you are not the woman in the photograph. Maybe you are someone else. But if you come to the office, I can see that you are the same person. Then I can give you a copy."

After work, Giselle goes to the newspaper office. When Milt sees her, he smiles. "Yes! You are the woman I photographed yesterday. I can send you the picture."

After dinner Giselle sits down at her computer. *I will send this picture to all my friends! I will say it was in the newspaper. I want to send it to my friend, Kathy,* she thinks. *Kathy said, 'I changed my mobile phone company and my Internet company.' She didn't tell me her new contact details. Maybe I can guess. Her old email address was kgrey@citymail.com. Her new company is superserver. So I think her new email address will be kgrey@superserver.com.*

She writes an email. She attaches the picture and sends it.

Forty kilometres away, in the next city, Keith Grey is checking his emails. He sees a new email in his inbox. He is the manager of a fashion store. He needs a new salesperson. He put an advertisement in the newspaper. He is waiting for emails from people who want the job.

So he is not surprised when he sees an email from someone he doesn't know. He opens the email.

---Look at this!

A photographer from our newspaper saw me in the street yesterday! He asked to take my photograph. It was in the Warmington newspaper this morning. I am so excited. Do you like it?

Love Giselle----

Keith looks at the picture. He likes it very much. *She is very pretty,* he thinks. *She looks very happy. I like her style. But she doesn't say anything about the job in my store. I don't understand. I think I will ask her to send more information.*

Giselle is very pleased when an email arrives from kgrey@superserver.com.

Kathy got my email! The address was correct!

She opens the email.

--- Dear Giselle,

Thank you very much for your email and picture. I like the picture very much. But if you want a job in my store, you must give me more information.

Regards,

Keith Grey

Manager, Pizazzy Fashion ---

Oh no! I sent my picture to a strange man! He will think I'm crazy. I don't want a new job!

Very quickly, Giselle sends an email back.

---Dear Mr Grey,

I am very sorry. It was a bad mistake. I wanted to send the picture to my friend Kathy. The email address was wrong.

I have a nice job and I am not looking for a new one.

Regards,

Giselle---

Keith reads Giselle's message. *It was a mistake. She doesn't want a job in my store. But I think she looks very nice. Does she have a boyfriend? Will she go on a date with me? How can I ask her?*

Keith thinks for a few minutes. He smiles. He finds a digital photograph of himself and he writes an email.

---Dear Giselle,

I will be in Warmington next Saturday. Will you please have coffee with me? I will be waiting at Sofrito Café at 11:00am. If you come, I will know who you are. I have your photograph!

And here is a photo of me.

Keith---

On Saturday, Keith is nervous. He is waiting at the door of the café. *Will she come? I hope so.*

He sees a young woman walking towards him. She has pink hair and she is wearing red boots. Today her skirt is black and white. She is smiling. She looks happy.

"Hi, Keith," she says. "I knew you from your photograph!"

4. NORIKO AND OLIVER

Oliver is looking for a shirt to wear to work.

Oh no! I don't have a clean shirt. I will have to wear a T-shirt. Today, it's OK, I don't have to meet anyone at the office. But tomorrow I have an important meeting. I need a smart shirt. I have to wash some clothes.

Oliver is American. He lives in Japan. He speaks Japanese very well. He works for a Japanese company.

He puts his dirty clothes in the washing machine and turns it on. He has a shower, makes coffee, eats breakfast and feeds his cat. He looks out the window of his house. *My clothes drier is broken, but it is windy today. My clothes will dry quickly outside.*

Before he leaves to catch the bus, he hangs his wet clothes on the line in the garden.

Oliver works hard all day. He doesn't think about the weather. He doesn't look at the weather news. He doesn't know that a typhoon is coming. The weather news says that the wind will be very, very strong and the rain will come about 7:00pm.

When he leaves his office, the wind is strong, but it is not raining. He takes the bus home. *I'll have noodles for dinner and maybe a beer,* he thinks. *Then I will iron all my shirts. When I have enough shirts for a week, I will watch baseball and I will have another beer.*

Oliver gets off the bus and walks to his house. He unlocks the door and goes into his house. He puts his briefcase on the floor. *I will get my clothes now,* he thinks.

He goes to the garden behind his house. He looks at the line. *Where are my clothes? What has happened?* When Oliver went to work, shirts and socks were hanging on the line. Now his clothes were gone.

Someone took my clothes! I must call the police.

Oliver calls the police station. "Someone came to my house. They took all my clothes!" he says.

"How did they get into your house?" asks a policeman.

"No. No one came into my house. My clothes were drying in the garden," says Oliver.

The policeman laughs. "It is very windy today. A typhoon is coming. Maybe the wind took your clothes."

"Uh, OK," says Oliver. "I'm sorry. I will look in my garden."

Oliver looks everywhere in his garden, but he can't find his clothes.

He thinks, *Maybe they flew to the house next door. I have to go and ask my neighbours if they saw my clothes. Maybe they will think I am crazy, but I have to find a shirt to wear to work tomorrow.*

Oliver checks the wind direction. *If my clothes flew away, they went that way. I don't know the people in that house.*

Now the wind is very strong, and it is raining hard. The weather is very noisy. It is difficult to walk. Oliver goes to the house next door and rings the bell.

A small boy comes to the door. The wind is so strong, the small boy cannot hold the door.

"Can I come in?" shouts Oliver.

The small boy doesn't answer, but Oliver holds the door and jumps into the house. He closes the door. Inside it is quieter.

"Is your mother home?" asks Oliver.

"No mother," says the small boy.

"Can I talk to your father?"

"No father."

What can I do? thinks Oliver.

"What is your name?" he asks the boy.

"Takeshi".

The house is shaking in the wind. Takeshi says, "Shoes." Oliver takes his shoes off. Takeshi takes his hand, and they walk from the entrance hall into the house.

There are two women in the kitchen. "Noriko san. Obaa-san," says Takeshi. He drops Oliver's hand. He picks up a toy truck from the floor and goes away.

The kitchen is warm. Oliver can smell delicious food. He looks at the two women.

"I'm sorry. My Japanese is not so good. I have lost my clothes. I washed my clothes this morning. When I came home from work, the clothes were not there. Can you help me?"

One of the women is very old. She smiles at Oliver. "Sit down," she says.

The other woman, Noriko, is young and very beautiful. "Your clothes came to our house," she says in English. "We found them in our garden. They were wet and dirty. Obaa-chan washed them again."

Oliver is panicking. He forgets how to speak Japanese.

"I need a shirt for work tomorrow! Only one. Can you give me one shirt? I have a very important meeting."

Noriko speaks to Obaa-san in Japanese.

"My grandmother says your clothes will not dry before tomorrow. But it is OK. She says there will be no buses or trains tomorrow. Maybe there will be no electricity. You will not have a meeting tomorrow. My grandmother is cooking dinner. Please stay and eat with us."

5. HELENA AND ANDERS

Sofia loved her grandparents. Everyone said, "They are the perfect couple." Today was a special day for Sofia's grandparents. It was their 60th wedding anniversary. All the family and their close friends were there.

The guests ate delicious food. They talked and laughed. Sofia's grandmother's name was Helena. She was 85 years old. She sat in a wheelchair because she could not walk well. She was a beautiful woman. Her hair and makeup were perfect. Sofia's grandfather's name was Anders. He was 87 years old. His hair was white.

At the end of the party, Sofia's father opened bottles of champagne and Sofia's mother carried a cake decorated with flowers to the table.

"Helena and Anders," said Sofia's father. "This is your party. We want you to make a speech."

Anders looked at Helena and smiled. He held her hand. "We are old. Nobody wants to listen to old people. We want the voices of young people. So we want Sofia to speak. Sofia, you are our youngest grandchild. What do you want to say?"

Everyone was looking at her. Sofia panicked. *What can I say? This is too difficult! I have to say something.*

"Uh! Uh! I love you. We all love you. You are amazing. But seeing you today, so much in love after sixty years, I have a question. Please tell us, how did you meet?"

"We met at a party in Vienna in nineteen fifty-nine," said Anders.

Helena looked at Anders. "No we didn't!" she said.

Everyone laughed. "You don't remember when you met!" said Sofia's father.

Anders laughed too. "Of course we remember. We were introduced at a party in Vienna, but we met for the first time in nineteen fifty-four."

Everyone at the party was surprised.

"Please tell us the story," said Sofia.

"Helena will tell you the story," said Anders.

"When I was a teenager, I went to a school for girls. It was a school for young ladies. It was very strict. We could not look at boys. We could not talk to boys. So we thought about boys all the time!

"When I was seventeen, I went from my school to my home in the mountains for Christmas," said Helena. "It was very exciting. It was the first time I was allowed to travel alone.

"The last part of my trip was on a very small local train. It went through many tunnels and across railway bridges. It was snowing very hard. I remember I was bored, because when I looked out the window, everything was white.

"Suddenly there were very loud bangs and noises and the train turned upside down! I couldn't understand what had happened. I was lying on the ceiling of the train. There were seats on top of me. I could hear screaming and shouting, but after a while, there was no sound at all. Everything was very quiet. There was no light. I couldn't see anything.

"I had no pain. I wasn't hurt, but I couldn't move. The seats were too heavy. I was trapped. I thought 'Maybe I am the only person alive. Maybe everyone on the train is dead'. I was very frightened.

"Then I heard someone moving. I said, 'Is someone there? Are you alive?' A man's voice came back. 'Yes. Where are you? Are you hurt?'

"I said, 'No. But the seats are on top of me and I can't move. Are you OK?'

The man answered, 'I think my leg is broken.'

"'What happened?' I asked. 'The train crashed,' he said. 'Don't worry. We must wait. Help will come.'

"We waited in the dark for hours. We talked. We talked about books. We talked about our plans for the Christmas vacation. We talked about our lives. He told me he was a university student. He was studying to be a doctor. It was the first time I ever spoke to a young man who wasn't my brother, or my cousin or a friend of my family.

"Finally, we could hear voices. There were lights and the sound of trucks and tractors. Everything happened very quickly. Men lifted the seats and carried me outside. My father came down the mountain when he heard about the train crash. He took me home. I was safe.

"Two years later, I finished school, and went home to help my mother in the house. I often thought about the young man on the train. It was my only adventure. In nineteen fifty-nine, my parents sent me to Vienna to stay with my aunt. It was time for me to go to parties and to meet a husband."

"Helena and her aunt came to a party at my boss's house," said Anders. "She was wearing a pink dress. I saw her come into the room. I thought, 'She is so beautiful!'

"I went to talk to her. But when I spoke, Helena said, 'The man from the train!'"

"Yes," said Helena. "I heard his voice. On the train I didn't see his face and he never told me his name. But I remembered his voice."

"And I remembered her voice," said Anders. "I never forgot the girl on the train. It was a wonderful surprise. The girl on the train was at a party in Vienna, wearing a pink dress!"

Anders smiled at everyone. "And that was how we met."

THANK YOU

Thank you for reading How Did You Meet? We hope you enjoyed it. (Word count: 4,562)

If you would like to read more graded readers, please visit our website http://www.italkyoutalk.com

Other Level 2 graded readers include
Adventure in Rome
Andre's Dream
A Passion for Music
Christmas Tales
Danger in Seattle
Don't Come Back
Elspeth and the Visitor
Finders Keepers…
John Sees a Murder
Marcy's Bakery
Men's Konkatsu Tales
Message in a Bottle
Murder in Marrakech
Murder on Whale Island
Salaryman Secrets!
Stories for Halloween
The Perfect Wedding
The House in the Forest

ABOUT THE AUTHOR

I Talk You Talk Press is an award-winning Japan-based publisher of language textbooks, graded readers and language learning/teaching resources. We won the Language Learner Literature Award in 2019 and 2020.

Our team is made up of highly experienced language teachers and translators, who have all studied at least one additional language to an advanced level.

This experience enables us to design our materials from the perspective of both the teacher and the learner. We consult with both teachers and language learners when designing our textbooks and graded readers, and test our materials extensively in the classroom before publication.

We are a fast-growing press, and currently publish graded readers for learners of English. We publish new graded readers monthly.

How Did You Meet?

How Did You Meet?

www.ingramcontent.com/pod-product-compliance
Lightning Source LLC
LaVergne TN
LVHW051517170726
843492LV00002B/979